JANE GOODALL

MASTERMINDS

IZZI HOWELL

WAYLAND

First published in Great Britain in 2020 by Wayland

Copyright © Hodder and Stoughton Limited, 2020

Produced for Wayland by
White-Thomson Publishing Ltd
www.wtpub.co.uk

Series Editor: Izzi Howell
Series Designer: Rocket Design (East Anglia) Ltd

HB ISBN: 978 1 5263 1268 6
PB ISBN: 978 1 5263 1269 3

Wayland
An imprint of
Hachette Children's Group
Part of Hodder & Stoughton
Carmelite House
50 Victoria Embankment
London EC4Y 0DZ

An Hachette UK Company
www.hachette.co.uk
www.hachettechildrens.co.uk

Printed in China

All words in bold appear in the glossary on page 30.

Picture acknowledgements:
Alamy: Danita Delimont cover, Steve Bloom Images 15, Everett Collection Inc 19, Minden Pictures 20, Liam White 21, Penny Tweedie 24; Getty: Michael Nichols 4b, Hulton Archive/Stringer 6 and 18t, anna1311 7, Bettmann 9, 17t and 22, CBS Photo Archive 12 and 13, Jonathan Kind 16–17, Duffy-Marie Arnoult 23 and 25, mihtiander 26, WPA Pool 28, Jeff Spicer/Stringer 29; Shutterstock: BOLDG 4t, Tinseltown 5 and 30, Volodymyr Burdiak 8, Marcio Jose Bastos Silva 10t, Puwadol Jaturawutthichai 10–11b, GUDKOV ANDREY 11t, Sam Dcruz 14, Susan Schmitz 18b, Ferenc Szelepcsenyi 27.
All design elements from Shutterstock.

CONTENTS

WHO IS JANE GOODALL?

Jane Goodall is a British **ethologist**. Her work has mainly focused on chimpanzees. She studied chimpanzees in the Gombe Stream National Park in Tanzania for over 20 years.

Africa

Tanzania is in the east of Africa

Jane was accepted by the chimpanzees and was able to live very near to them. This allowed her to **observe** them closely.

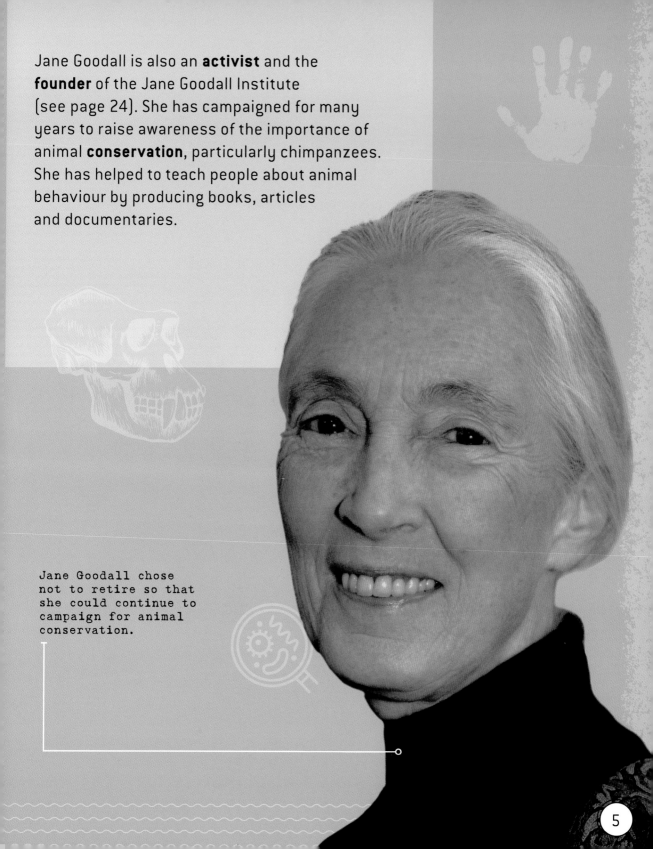

Jane Goodall is also an **activist** and the **founder** of the Jane Goodall Institute (see page 24). She has campaigned for many years to raise awareness of the importance of animal **conservation**, particularly chimpanzees. She has helped to teach people about animal behaviour by producing books, articles and documentaries.

Jane Goodall chose not to retire so that she could continue to campaign for animal conservation.

Jane was born in London, UK, on 3 April 1934. Her father, Mortimer, was a businessman and her mother, Margaret, wrote novels. Four years later, Jane's younger sister Judith was born. Jane had a happy childhood and loved playing outside and exploring. She often found school boring, as she really wanted to be outdoors in nature.

When she was one year old, Jane's father gave her a toy chimpanzee similar to this one. Jane loved the toy, which she named Jubilee.

Jane was fascinated by animals as a child. She had many pets, including cats, hamsters and guinea pigs. She read many books about wild animals and dreamed of seeing wildlife in Africa one day.

Jane's parents encouraged her interests. Her mother told her that she could achieve anything she wanted by working hard and never giving up.

One of Jane's first animal **research** projects was trying to find out where eggs come from. She spent hours in her family's henhouse, observing the chickens.

OFF TO AFRICA

Jane left school at 18. She worked as a secretary and at a film production company. In 1957, Jane's dream of visiting Africa came true when she went on a trip to Kenya. She was invited to visit a school friend's family farm.

Jane was finally able to see the wildlife of Africa for herself during her trip to Kenya.

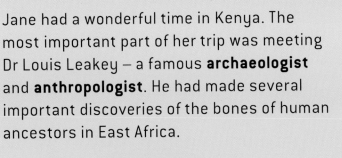

Jane had a wonderful time in Kenya. The most important part of her trip was meeting Dr Louis Leakey – a famous **archaeologist** and **anthropologist**. He had made several important discoveries of the bones of human ancestors in East Africa.

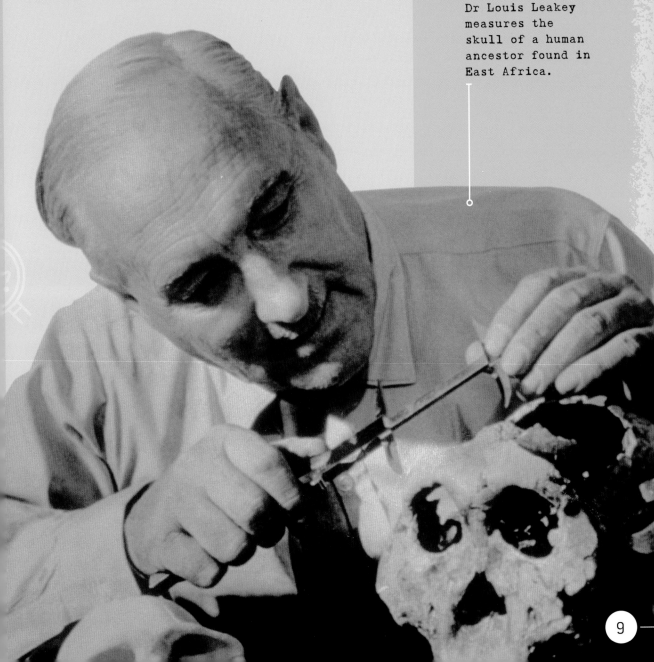

Dr Louis Leakey measures the skull of a human ancestor found in East Africa.

Dr Louis Leakey's discovery of the remains of human ancestors proved that human **evolution** had taken place in Africa. Millions of years ago, humans and **primates** evolved separately from the same ancestor.

This is a model of a Neanderthal - a separate species of human that lived at the same time as early modern humans. Today, around 2 per cent of our DNA can be traced back to Neanderthals.

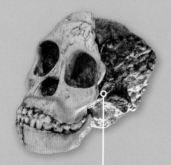

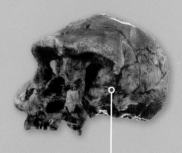

AUSTRALOPITHECUS
lived 4.4 to 1.4 million years ago

HOMO ERECTUS
lived 1.9 million to 200,000 years ago

As no direct human ancestors survive, primates, and in particular chimpanzees, are the closest living species to humans. Dr Louis Leakey thought that understanding chimpanzees would help him get a better understanding of how human ancestors lived, so he asked Jane to study them.

Chimpanzees form complex social groups, just like humans. Some members of the group are more **dominant** and control the other chimpanzees.

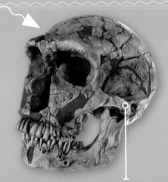

HOMO NEANDERTHALENSIS
lived 200,000 to 35,000 years ago

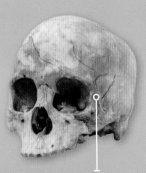

HOMO SAPIENS
evolved around 315,000 years ago

Over time, the ancestors of humans evolved to have larger brains, and therefore larger skulls. They developed spoken language and the ability to understand complex ideas.

In June 1960, Jane set up a camp in what is now the Gombe Stream National Park. She studied the chimpanzees in their natural habitat. She gave names to the chimpanzees that she observed, such as Flo and David Greybeard.

Jane watched the chimpanzees from a distance until she had gained their trust.

Jane observed many young chimpanzees and their relationships with their siblings, parents and other members of the group.

Jane spent a lot of time taking notes on the chimpanzees' social behaviour. She understood them as individuals, and saw their role and place in the group's **hierarchy**. Jane observed that each chimpanzee had its own personality, emotions and relationships with other members of the group.

NEW DISCOVERIES

Jane quickly began observing behaviour that challenged previous ideas about how chimpanzees act. Before, people had believed that chimpanzees were almost entirely vegetarian.

However, Jane discovered that chimpanzees were actually **omnivores** and ate both plants and other animals. She observed chimpanzees hunting together for larger animals, such as jungle pigs.

Fruit makes up a large part of a chimpanzee's diet, but we now know that they also eat meat, thanks to Jane's research.

Jane's most important discovery happened when she observed one of the chimpanzees, David Greybeard, making a tool. He stripped leaves from a twig to make a tool to fish termites (insects) out of a nest.

Previously, it was thought that humans were the only species that used tools. Since then, we have discovered other species that also use tools, including other primates, sea otters and crows.

tool

This group of chimpanzees is gathering termites from a nest using stick tools.

termite nest

Although Jane was a skilled researcher, she didn't have any formal training and had never been to university. So in 1962, she started studying for a **PhD** in ethology at Cambridge University in the UK.

Jane's time studying at Newnham College at Cambridge University was a big change from her time living with chimpanzees in Tanzania.

Jane went back and forth between the UK and Tanzania to continue the research for her PhD. She graduated in 1965. She is one of very few people to have completed a PhD without having been to university for another **degree** first.

The group of chimpanzees in Gombe were the subject of Jane's PhD.

FAMILY

In 1964, Jane married a Dutch photographer called Hugo van Lawick. They met when Hugo came to Tanzania to film Jane's work. His films and photos helped to make Jane's research famous around the world.

Hugo filmed Jane's research. As well as chimpanzees, Jane went on to study other primates, such as baboons.

baboon

In 1967, Jane and Hugo had a son. They named him Hugo, after his father, but called him by his nickname Grub. In 1974, Hugo and Jane divorced, but they remained friends.

Jane got remarried in 1975 to Derek Bryceson. He worked in the Tanzanian government and in national parks. Sadly, Derek died five years later in 1980.

Grub (Hugo) travelled with his parents to different areas where they were doing research or filming.

In 1965, Jane set up a training centre in Gombe. She wanted to help other students who were interested in studying primates. Many people, both men and women, trained at the centre. It had previously been unusual for women to work as **primatologists**, but thanks to Jane, it became more common.

Today, many women work as primatologists and in a huge number of other science fields too.

After Jane's study of chimpanzees, Dr Louis Leakey asked two other women to study primates. Dian Fossey (1932–1985) studied gorillas in Rwanda and Biruté Galdikas (1946–) studied orangutans in Borneo. The research of both women helped to raise awareness of the importance of protecting primates.

Dian Fossey lived closely with gorillas and studied their relationships and behaviour.

TIONAL PRESS CLUB

Jane's work has helped to get people interested in chimpanzees. She believes that if people understand chimpanzees and their behaviour, they will be motivated to work to protect them.

Jane worked with the World Wildlife Fund charity in 1985 on a campaign to help protect primates.

Jane celebrated the launch of one of her books in 2009.

JANE GOODALL
with Thane Maynard *and* Gail Hudson
Hope for Animals

Jane has written books about her time with chimpanzees, such as *In the Shadow of Man* and *Through a Window*. These books became very popular, as people were fascinated by the characters of the different chimpanzees in Gombe. One chimpanzee, Flo, was so well-loved that a newspaper published an **obituary** of her when she died.

THE JANE GOODALL INSTITUTE

In 1977, Jane set up the Jane Goodall Institute (JGI). The team at the Jane Goodall Institue continue her research in Gombe, as well as working to protect chimpanzees and their habitats in other areas.

The Jane Goodall Institute also supports other conservation projects across Africa. Here, one of the founders of the JGI in Uganda poses with one of the chimpanzees under their protection.

Jane has also set up a youth programme called Roots and Shoots. This organisation helps to engages young people with conservation issues and inspires them to grow up to be leaders and activists.

Jane Goodall attends a Roots and Shoots event in New York City, USA.

ACTIVISM

Jane is passionate about raising awareness of the threats facing wild animals. Chimpanzees are currently an endangered species. This is because their forest habitat is often cut down to create farmland or to use the trees for wood. This leaves the chimpanzees without food or shelter. Chimpanzees are also sometimes killed for their meat, or caught to be sold as pets.

When a forest is cut down, every plant and animal that lives there is made homeless or killed.

Jane travels approximately 300 days a year to make speeches and attend events around the world. She believes that it is important for us to act now to save the environment to preserve these species for the future.

Jane shares her experiences and research to inspire others to protect the environment and the animals that live there.

CELEBRATING JANE GOODALL

Jane Goodall's **pioneering** work and dedication to activism and conservation have been celebrated in many ways. She has received multiple awards and was made a **Dame** in 2003. In 2019, Jane was named one of the 100 most influential people in the world by *Time* magazine.

Jane Goodall meeting Queen Elizabeth II in 2012.

In 2017, a biographical documentary was made about Jane Goodall's life. The film, *Jane*, contained footage from the whole of Jane's career, covering her important and pioneering research and activism.

Jane Goodall attended several screenings of the film *Jane* when it was released.

GLOSSARY

activist – someone who tries to change society or politics

anthropologist – someone who studies human development and society

archaeologist – someone who studies the past by looking at the remains of ancient objects and people

conservation – protecting nature

Dame – a title in the UK for a woman given for valuable work

degree – a qualification you receive after finishing a university course

dominant – describes someone or something that is strong and in control

ethologist – someone who studies animal behaviour

evolution – the way in which living things change gradually over millions of years

founder – someone who starts an organisation

hierarchy – a system in which people are organised according to their importance

obituary – a report in a newspaper about the life of someone who has recently died

observe – to watch something carefully

omnivore – an animal that eats both plants and meat

PhD – the most advanced qualification from a university

pioneering – starting the development of something important

primate – a group of animals including chimpanzees, gorillas and orangutans

primatologist – someone who studies primates

research – studying something in order to get more information about it

TIMELINE

1934
Jane is born in London, UK.

1957
Jane travels to Kenya and meets Dr Louis Leakey.

1960
Jane sets up camp in the Gombe Stream National Park.

1962
Jane starts studing for a PhD in ethology at Cambridge University.

1964
Jane marries Hugo van Lawick.

1965
Jane completes her PhD and graduates.

FURTHER INFORMATION

BOOKS

Animal Families: Chimpanzees
by Tim Harris
(Wayland, 2014)

Brilliant Women: Pioneers of Science and Technology
by Georgia Amson-Bradshaw
(Wayland, 2019)

Dynamic Duos of Science: Jane Goodall and Mary Leakey
by Matt Anniss
(Franklin Watts, 2016)

WEBSITES

www.janegoodall.org
Learn more about the Jane Goodall Institute and the work it does around the world.

www.rootsandshoots.org
Find out about Roots and Shoots – Jane Goodall's youth conservation programme.

vimeo.com/5000150
Watch a video from the Jane Goodall Institute about how chimpanzees learn from each other.

1965
Jane sets up a training centre for primatologists in Gombe.

1967
Hugo (Grub), Jane and Hugo's son, is born.

1977
The Jane Goodall Institute is set up.

2003
Jane is made a Dame.

2017
A biographical documentary is made about Jane's life.

2019
Jane is named one of the 100 most influential people in the world by *Time* magazine.

INDEX